**LESLIE GREENE**

# HOME LEARNING

**The Essential Guide to a Successful Home School Program
For Your Child, Discover Effective Home School Strategies
That Would Make Learning at Home a Breeze!**

**Descrierea CIP a Bibliotecii Naţionale a României**
**LESLIE GREENE**
    **HOME LEARNING. The Essential Guide to a Successful Home School Program For Your Child, Discover Effective Home School Strategies That Would Make Learning at Home a Breeze!** / Leslie Greene – Bucharest: Editura My Ebook, 2021
    ISBN

**LESLIE GREENE**

# HOME LEARNING

**The Essential Guide to a Successful Home School Program
For Your Child, Discover Effective Home School Strategies
That Would Make Learning at Home a Breeze!**

My Ebook Publishing House
Bucharest, 2021

# TABLE OF CONTENTS

# INTRODUCTION

Regardless of your reasons for wanting to home school, one of the questions that is probably burning in your mind is:

### *Do I have what it takes to be an effective teacher?*

Will your children buckle down and get the work done? Can you get rid of the distractions in their lives so they can learn and focus more easily? How do you separate family time from school time so it's well balanced?

And how will you still find time to complete your own personal tasks each day while still being available to your child?

One of the first things you need to keep in mind is to be a parent first and an educator second. Your kids are going to need Mom or Dad to love them, listen to them, and play with them.

Yes, you can do these things while they're learning once you get the hang of things, but have those as your priorities, especially when you're just starting out. That doesn't mean school isn't as important, but it does mean they need to realize that first of all, you're Mom or Dad (or Grandma, Grandpa, whatever the case may be.

They should feel free to come to you with their problems instead of worrying you'll get upset or frustrated because they need extra help.

Remember, this is a transition for both you and your child and it will require commitment, dedication and above all else, patience!

Here are ten tips you can follow that will allow you to home school without losing your marbles.

Let's begin!

# Create a Reasonable Plan

In order to be successful with home schooling your child, you need to create a plan of action. Your child's school may be able to provide you with a curriculum you can follow. This might include worksheets, workbooks, or educational websites your child will need to use in order to complete specific tasks or assignments.

If you're lucky enough to have the school's help, your main job will be to make sure everyone's participating, everything's getting done on time, and everyone understands the lessons.

If your school isn't all that involved, don't panic. Yes, you'll be making up your own lesson plans, but you'll still have plenty of help. You want to base your plans around your child's grade level, their skills and abilities, and on the work they were doing at school (if you can find that out).

Run a Google search for your child's grade level and your State's Board of Education to find learning goals for each of their subjects. You'll want to concentrate on "The Three R's" (reading, writing, and arithmetic AKA language arts and math) of course, but remember not to neglect the other courses. Your child will benefit from a solid knowledge of science or history, as well as the creativity taught by the arts.

There are plenty of online sources that can help as well. You can download entire textbooks, worksheets, workbooks, and lesson plans. You can also get involved in Facebook groups dedicated to home schooling, if you need help or feel you'd benefit from the encouragement from other parents who may be facing the same challenges.

In addition, use Google to find language and math websites that offer online lessons or extra learning practice. Your local library can also be a lifesaver. Get to know your librarian and find out what kinds of resources they may offer!

Talk to your child's public school teachers and find out where they obtain the materials they use to teach with. There are plenty of good resources you can use in your classroom, and we'll talk about some of them in this special report. Teachers can help you learn where to find these resources and which ones will actually work.

One thing about lesson plans: make sure your objectives are something concrete that you can measure.

For example, you want them to "be able to count to ten" instead of "be able to know addition," to "recite a short poem" instead of "appreciate poetry."

## Establish a Daily Routine

You're probably not going to be able to schedule a routine in the same way the public school did, however it's important that you create some sort of structure that will make it easier on both you and your child.

Establishing a routine will help your child know what to expect, it'll help you plan out your day so you have the time you need for your own work or activities, and it will create a clear divide between personal time and school time (which will help your child stay focused!)

It's usually best to take care of *your* schedule first, then see where the homeschooling will fit into that. That way you're focused and able to dedicate the time to helping your child with their school work, free from distraction.

When you're homeschooling, it's important that you and your kids follow a bedtime and wake-up routine as well. They should try to wake up at the same time every day and change into "work clothes" instead of lounging around in their pajamas.

That way your child is retaining a similar schedule and routine that they did when they were attending school.

You, too, should lead by example, being dressed and ready in time for classes. Create a daily routine that everyone follows. You won't have the traditional 8:00 to 3:00 schedule (with recess between classes!) but you should have some sort of set routine.

School begins and ends on time, and you'll be working during that time, not playing with cellphones or listening to the TV in the other room. Your child will only be as invested as you are!

Remember, younger kids and teens need at least 10 hours of sleep in order to perform at their best. And sadly, most kids (and their parents!) are chronically sleep-deprived, which makes a big difference in their ability to learn. So, try to get them to bed at a decent hour so they can get that much-needed rest.

Having a set daily routine benefits everyone in the family. Your kids will get used to being "in school" at a certain time and will therefore be far more focused and ready to learn.

You will also have the ability to plan your day more effectively and utilizing your time the best way possible. In addition, it's a lot easier to work diligently based on a set schedule or daily plan, than just to "wing it".

## Assign a Dedicated Learning Space

You already know how easily kids can get distracted. If you're lucky enough to have a separate room you can use for school, that's fantastic. If, like most of us, you're forced to work in a corner of the living room, work with what you've got! It's totally okay: the goal is to assign a dedicated learning space and stick with it.

That way, your kids know that once they're within that area, it's time to get to work.

You'll need somewhere for everyone to sit where they can spread their work out and write or work online. The kitchen or dining room table will work, as will a desk, if they have one. If you've got several kids and only one computer, of course, they're going to have to take turns with that. But if you've got enough tablets or laptops for everyone, even better!

Note: if your kid would rather sprawl on the floor to work, that's fine too. Whatever gets the job done. Don't forget to save a place for the teacher.

If you can't spare the table for the entire duration of the home- school day (maybe you need to prepare lunch or use the desk for a teleconference), get a basket for the school supplies and let the kids carry them to a secondary space, but whenever possible, staying within a space dedicated to school work will help them stay focused.

You'll also want to do your best to eliminate distractions. Turn the TV and cellphones off (you should probably put the phones away completely so they're not even tempted).

Make sure the pets are excluded from the room. Tell your friends and coworkers what time you're teaching so they don't interrupt with calls or visits.

If you'd like some background music, science has shown that soft instrumental music helps kids concentrate best (no lyrics or heavy beats).

You might even want to put up a "Work in Progress" sign like you see in offices so that other family members know not to disturb you when "school" is in session. Write out the times you'll be holding class each day and add "Do Not Disturb" to the sign.

If everyone knows that this is the designated school room, you're far more likely to get a good day's work out of your students.

## Prepare Your Learning Tools

You'll want to do your best to stay very organized when home schooling. Have everything you and your children will need ready to go every day.

Create or download your lesson plans ahead of time so you know what you'll be doing and can give yourself a quick refresher course if you need help with any of the day's concepts.

Have your materials laid out before you need them. Make sure the kids have no excuse to stop working at any time.

One good organizational tool is to make a syllabus for each child. This doesn't have to be a complicated document. Buy a cheap folder and print out their weekly schedule, with a space for them to check off or color in when they have finished each assignment.

That way, they can see what work is due on which day, and what they're going to be working on during the week. You can even allow them to "play around" with the schedule and work at their own pace, so long as everything is completed by the end of the week.

You can make up a "Google doc" for the schedule, with days of the week as columns. Your rows will be the subject and resources needed for each day's work.

Put a little circle (or star or whatever icon you wish) in the right row to show what needs doing on which day. Your kids can color that icon in when the job's done.

For example, you might have Language Arts on Monday, Tuesday, and Thursday, with resources being their workbook on Monday, online class Tuesday, and writing practice book Thursday.

Not only does this keep your kids from asking "What do I do now?" all day long, but it lets you know what's been done and what you need to help them with.

If you have materials for the day's lessons, be sure those are prepared and laid out before the kids arrive. There's nothing that disrupts a lesson faster than having a last-minute hunt for crayons or workbooks.

If you're using online lesson plans, make sure you've logged on ahead of time to be sure the connection works and will play properly on your computer.

Plan for variety, too. Use workbooks for subjects like writing or math, so the kids can physically write their answers out. Let them doodle in the margins, too, if that helps them work better.

Utilize online classes, apps, videos, etc. for harder concepts in math, science, and history. And try printable resources like notebooks digital graphic tablets to tempt them into working on their handwriting and spelling.

Flash cards are a tried and true method, and there are plenty of educational games you can find or borrow from the library. And don't forget the "old standbys" – pens, pencils, paper, white board and markers. Mix it up and you'll have a more interested group of kids.

If you're organized, your kids will learn more easily. They'll also see that being organized helps, so they'll be more likely to start organizing things themselves. You can let them help you get organized, too.

Have them help you download their workbook and print it out, or let the older kids find the right materials for tomorrow's class with the younger ones.

## Take Breaks

Working straight through anything can be exhausting. Imagine going your entire work shift without a lunch or stretch break. Kids often get tired even faster than you do because their minds are still learning to focus for longer periods of time. The traditional school schedule, with forty- to fifty-minute classes followed by a short break, was designed that way for a reason.

That doesn't mean your kids need to take a break every ten minutes, however you should always plan breaks throughout the day.

For smaller children, twenty to thirty minutes of study followed by a five- or ten-minute break is ideal. Older kids can go an entire fifty minutes without stopping. During their break, encourage your kids to get up and move around, too. Exercise helps get the blood circulating to the brain, which will wake the kids up and get them thinking more effectively.

Every two to four hours (depending on what tasks you've got planned), take a longer break – maybe thirty minutes. Use that as a "recess." Try to get the kids outside running around, using up all that excess energy so they'll be ready to get back to work again.

Explain the schedule to your kids beforehand, so they know they'll have a break coming up and will be less likely to squirm in their seats or lose focus. If they realize they're only working for a short time, or in bursts, they'll be far more likely to buckle down and get the work done. And if they start getting antsy, you can remind them they only have to work for a bit longer.

Your school day might be a bit longer or shorter than a public  school day, but regardless, with frequent breaks your kids will be more likely to stay engaged for the entire day, and they'll certainly be able to concentrate better.

You can assure them that this method works for study time as well: study for twenty to thirty minutes, then go take a five- or ten-minute break before you hit the books  again.

## Social Interaction

One downside of homeschooling is that the kids may end up feeling isolated. They don't have that interaction with their friends that they're used to, and there's no one else to talk to between classes.

You're likely to feel isolated as well, especially if this is your first home schooling experience. It's easy to become overwhelmed and feel you're all alone in this. The way around this problem is to keep in touch with your community.

*Who's your community?*

For your kids, it's their peers – either their former classmates or kids their own age or kids in the neighborhood. For you, it's other parents, especially those who are also homeschooling.

Encourage your kids to video chat with their peers. They may already be using Skype or FaceTime, but why not add a

Zoom meeting so they can discuss their lessons or help each other with homework?

If they can't have a sleepover, maybe they can have a virtual party together. It's easy for kids to feel isolated if they can't see or talk to their friends and school mates. You can help them deal with this by using the technology available.

When it comes to you, run a Google search for homeschooling communities. You can usually find something in your town or even neighborhood. There are plenty of online communities as well. You might even have a Facebook page for local home- schoolers where you can "get together" and share ideas (and struggles!).

Try the Zoom idea with this as well. Arrange a virtual meeting with other home-schooling adults, either from your neighborhood or with kids the same basic ages. Share lesson plans or study ideas. Brainstorm how to get that difficult concept across to the kids.

The whole idea is to see that none of you are alone in this. There are literally millions of other parents and kids who are home- schooling. Everyone faces challenges and difficulties at times. Get in contact with some of these people and be open to sharing your home-schooling experiences. You'll feel much better if you do.

# Get Them Moving

Your kids (and you) should be getting out of your seats every thirty to fifty minutes (See the earlier chapter called "Take Breaks"). Don't just stand there like lumps – get moving! Get that blood circulating to your brain so you're more alert and learning new things will become easier.

You can even include physical exercise as a class of its own! Of course, you're not going to be able to play sports without a full team, but you can work on your moves and practice the routines. You can also play games like tag or tug of war. You can have agility-increasing games like racing while holding a boiled egg in a spoon in your mouth, or three-legged races, or even Twister.

The idea is to get moving! Kids, especially, need physical activity. Their muscles and bones are still growing, and they need to learn how to move them in a coordinated fashion. They're still learning how to control and use their bodies, and they need lots of practice. They've also got a lot of pent-up energy they need to get rid of.

Spend your short breaks doing aerobics like jumping jacks, running in place, sprints, or gymnastic stunts. Every two to four hours, take a longer break and play active games with your kids. Make sure they're using up that energy and getting their blood moving. Encourage rowdiness to a certain degree – they shouldn't be tearing anything up, but they should be active, energetic kids.

You need the exercise as well. Not only is teaching a mostly sedentary job, but you, too, can get sluggish concentrating on one thing for so long. So, get out there and do those jumping jacks with the kids. Practice your yoga while they're sprinting, or take up tai chi while they have a scavenger hunt.

You'll find, if you get them moving now and then, you'll have a more attentive and more alert group of students afterwards.

Wake their brains up and you'll be surprised as what they can accomplish.

# Use Manipulatives

Manipulatives are physical items that your kids can handle and manipulate in order to learn. Most of these will be helpful in learning math, but you can use your imagination and see what you can accomplish in other subjects as well

You don't have to spend a lot of money to find manipulatives you can use with your students. You've got plenty of items already in your home that you can use with a little imagination.

For example, a little sand in a Tupperware sandwich container makes a dandy writing tray for practicing their letters. Any small items can be used to count, add or subtract, create groups and study fractions.

You'll probably want to invest in a good set of base ten blocks. These are blocks that break down (or build up) by tens so kids can learn to add, subtract, multiply and divide by physically manipulating the blocks into groups. You can usually find a good set, made of washable and durable plastic, for between $20 to $50 on Amazon.

You'll want a clock, too. You can get a cheap one at the Dollar Store or even make one yourself. Not only do you want your kids to learn how to tell time, but with a physical clock, you can teach them how long seconds and minutes are, and how to add and subtract time. Kids learn more easily when they can actually see the clock's hands measuring time out for them.

Another useful manipulative is a set of dice. You can either get "regular" six-sided dice or invest in a set of those multiple-sided ones used in role-playing games.

Dice are useful for playing printable math games as well as practicing their math facts. Roll two dice and add/subtract/multiply/divide the results. Roll two dice and write out a math fact using the numbers (2<5). For small children, try buying a set of over-sized foam dice to make math more fun.

Fraction tiles are also helpful when trying to visualize a difficult concept. These tiles – you can get magnetic ones! – show how different fractions fit together to make a whole. Sure, you can get the same result by cutting their sandwich into different fractions, but tiles are less messy than a PB&J. You can get a good set for under $20.

I'll bet you have a set of playing cards around the house somewhere. These are useful not only for math facts (like using dice), but also for playing various math card games (you can do a Google search for any number of these).

There are just so many additional manipulatives out there: 3D shapes, hundreds charts, play money, pattern blocks – you might have trouble reining yourself in once you start looking at everything that's out there to help your kids learn.

## Include Their Interests

Your kids are individuals. They have their own likes and dislikes, their own skills and talents. If you use your imagination, you can tie those interests into what you're teaching and help them learn even faster.

For example, let's say your kid's fascinated by dinosaurs. For a writing exercise, have them trace the letters of the dinosaur names (for younger kids) or write a report on their favorite type of dinosaur.

For math, use the dinosaur toys to show how addition and subtraction works, or illustrate fractions of a whole group.

For history, they can memorize the dates their dinosaurs walked the earth or learn when various fossils were first discovered.

Science, of course, would directly study the anatomy and physiology of the animals.

The idea is, if you are just a little creative, you can use their interests to "hook" them into learning more. If you can create a connection between a harder subject and one they're interested in, they'll learn more easily and remember facts longer.

*Here are some ways to "think outside the box" with your school subjects.*

- *Math* – play games, work puzzles, use manipulatives, plan a budget or save up for something, map out a garden, plan a menu, follow a cooking recipe, sew something using a pattern, learn woodworking.

- *Language Arts* – play language games, read books on their subject of interest, watch documentaries or films about that subject, write a journal about what they've learned, write and perform a play or skit, write and illustrate a report, copy and learn new words, make up a story about their subject.

- *Science and Nature* – watch documentaries and films, go on field trips to farms or dairies or zoos, join 4-H, take care of a pet, make a bird feeder and record visitors, study the weather, take a nature walk, read a field guide, make a leaf or rock collection, put together a model or robot, raise butterflies or tadpoles, have a science fair, play science games, create an experiment.

- *History* – go to a museum or heritage site, watch a documentary, play history games, watch and discuss the news, read a newspaper, make a timeline, read history books, study other cultures, watch historical films, dress up as a historical character, prepare a recipe from an old cookbook, learn traditional songs, interview an elderly person

- *Art* – go to an art gallery, learn music or songs about their subject of interest, draw or paint or sculpt their subject, read about an artist or their work, watch a documentary or film about an artist or art movement, make a chalk mural, make a collage about their subject, learn the math behind art.

# Take the Class Outside

If you're looking to change things up and recharge both yourself and your student, go breathe some fresh air and get some Vitamin D by being out in the sunlight. Take a brisk walk and do some exercises. Get your blood flowing and your brain working actively again.

There are many ways and reasons to take your school day outside. You can take a nature walk and learn what plants and animals live in your neighborhood. You can go to the nearest park and start a leaf collection, or measure the playground equipment. You can set up a weather station in your yard and keep records. You can learn how to march in time or do acrobatics or gymnastics. You can set up a bird feeder and record your visitors.

You can also plan outings for your students. Go to the zoo. Visit a museum. See an art gallery. Hike the local trails. See a play. Visit a national or state park. Run a Google search for activities in your town and see what's available. I'll bet you'll be surprised what's out there you can take advantage of!

See if your town has any historical sites you can visit. Even an old cemetery can provide opportunities to learn history and practice art (tombstone rubbings) or math (plotting the graves). You might be surprised to find a historic house that offers tours, though, or a heritage site you can visit. The local courthouse is a great place to learn politics and law, and you might even be able to tour the police or fire station.

Check out your local community services as well. Volunteer to help the local Red Cross. Check out the local animal shelter, too, and see if they have a program where kids can read to the animals. Visit a pottery studio.

Try arranging a visit to a possible career site like a dog groomer, the bakery, a factory, the dentist's office, a travel agent, the local photography studio, the veterinarian, or a real estate office.

Outings don't necessarily have to be strictly educational, either. You can use your creativity and rationalize a trip to the movie theater, symphony or concert, holiday performances or festival, skating rink, bowling alley, ball park, or amusement park.

So long as you're getting out of the house, it counts. Try to make  it educational, but even if it's not, make memories with your kids. That's what's important.

# CONCLUSION

Home schooling is an enormous endeavor, and it requires planning and discipline in order to stay on track. If you follow the tips included in this special report, it'll be much easier on all of you, and you may even really enjoy the experience!

Remember, the key is to create a schedule, stay organized and develop a reasonable routine. Minimize distractions by assigning a dedicated learning space. Do your best to remain patient and always keep in mind that this is as much of a transition to your child as it is to you.

It'll take some time and dedication, but it could end up being one of the most rewarding experiences of your life.

To your success!

# RESOURCES

Here are links to a few resources that I believe will help you:

**Home Schooling Tips:**

>> https://thesurvivalmom.com/my-top-16-tips-for-beginning- homeschoolers/

**Home School Success:**

>> https://www.scholastic.com/parents/school-success/school- involvement/8-steps-to-homeschool-success.html

**Home Schooling Made Easy:**

>> https://www.prodigygame.com/main-en/blog/5-effective- homeschooling-tips-for-parents/

## Establishing a Schedule:

>>https://www.goodhousekeeping.com/life/g33010658/homeschoo l-ideas/

Printed by Libri Plureos GmbH in Hamburg, Germany